Thunder Bay Press
An imprint of the Baker & Taylor Publishing Group
10350 Barnes Canyon Road, San Diego, CA 92121
www.thunderbaybooks.com

Text by Josephine Collins, copyright © Little Tiger Press 2013
Illustrations copyright © Jill Latter 2013
Jill Latter has asserted her right to be identified as the illustrator
of this work under the Copyright, Designs and Patents Act, 1988

All notations of errors or omissions should be addressed to Thunder Bay Press,
Editorial Department, at the above address. All other correspondence (author
inquiries, permissions) concerning the content of this book should be addressed to
Little Tiger Press, 1 The Coda Centre, 189 Munster Road, London SW6 6AW

ISBN-13: 978-1-62686-092-6
ISBN-10: 1-62686-092-0

Printed in China.
LTP/1800/0868/1213

1 2 3 4 5 17 16 15 14 13

My Wonderful Daughter

THUNDER BAY
P·R·E·S·S
SAN DIEGO

Daughter, you are...

so beautiful,

so clever,

so surprising,

so *wonderful!*

To have **YOU** as my daughter and my friend...

makes me the *happiest* person alive.

You only have to *smile*...

and my day is PERFECT!

I remember...

telling stories and laughing with you...

building forts and hiding with you...

dressing up and dancing with you!

Memories of *special* times.

It seems only yesterday that you were my little girl,

skipping along...

Now, LOVELY daughter, you are a beautiful woman,

dancing on her way!

From your **FIRST** smile,

your first step, your first word…

you have been — and always will be —

the *sunshine* in my world.

For ALL the fun and *messy* times,

the *magic* and the make-believe,

the laughter and *giggly* silliness...

thank you, my darling.

I love the *little* things you do!

If ever you're AFRAID,

I'll be there to *hold* your hand.

No matter how far away you are,

I *still* feel close to YOU.

ALWAYS cheering you on...

always on your side...

always there for a hug…

I'm always there for you,

my daughter.

I LOVE cooking you your *favorite* things!

Laughing *together*...

chatting together...

HAPPY together!

Daughter, may you believe that **ANYTHING** is possible...

and may **ALL** your dreams come *true!*

You ALWAYS know how to *cheer* me up.

For all the messages and *wishes* you send me,

and all the KIND things you do...

thank you, lovely daughter!

Seeing you now,

so GROWN-UP,

so brave, so *kind*...

makes me so proud.

Sometimes I just want to SHOUT OUT –

and tell the whole world how *amazing* you are!

I hope you know how SPECIAL you are...

how loved you are...

wonderful,

wonderful daughter!